Hello, little duckling!
How do you do?

Ducklings love…
waddling on their webby feet…oops!

Even though they sometimes
fall flat on their faces!

Ducklings love…
walking in a line…

fishing in a muddy pond…

drinking from a birdbath...

jumping off a dock. Splash!

Ducklings love...
making friends with puppy dogs...

fuzzy chicks,

and bunny rabbits.

Ducklings love sleeping all cozy
with their beaks
tucked under their wings.

Ducklings love swimming after
bread scraps.
"Quack! Quack! More, please!"

Ducklings love nestling in a basket because...